C000242361

EXPLORING SILENCE

WENDY ROBINSON

SLG Press

Convent of the Incarnation Fairacres
Parker Street Oxford OX4 1TB England

www.slgpress.co.uk

First published by SLG Press, 1974

Third edition 2013

Cover illustration
Icon of the 'Perfect' Silence
© *Wendy Robinson*

ISBN: 978-0-7283-0237-2
ISSN: 0307-1405

Printed by:
Will Print Oxford England

CONTENTS

ICON OF THE 'PERFECT' SILENCE

About the cover image

The form of this icon appeared in sixteenth-century Russia. Sometimes called 'Our Saviour of the Blessed Silence', it is an image, or icon, of the 'perfect' silence shown to us by Christ, revealing to us the One whom we seek in contemplative, monastic, ascetic, silent prayer. It helps us to quieten our spirit and deepen the prayer of silence before God.

The Messiah is shown as a winged youth in royal robes with hands crossed, and without the usual book or scroll. He is the Angel of God's Presence[1] and is linked with the passage:

The Spirit of wisdom and understanding,
The Spirit of counsel and might,
The Spirit of knowledge and of the fear of the Lord.[2]

The halo reveals that it is a messianic Christ icon. The Cross of the Resurrected Christ's victory over death is shown in the halo. The Incarnation is shown in the superimposed quadrilaterals. The dark blue represents heaven, and the red represents earth: the two natures of Christ in one Person. The fourth corner of the 'heavenly' quadrilateral is hidden, the eighth corner of the whole. It represents the Eighth Day, known only by the Father, not by human beings or angels.

Silence is shown in the crossed hands of receptive non-action; in the general portrayal of patience and long-suffering, gifts of the Spirit; and in an atmosphere of blessed silence. The icon draws us into the silence, calls us to deepen our silent prayer in Christ, and leaves us with the awesome responsibility of our created freedom to choose and to follow in joyful assent and in times of affliction: '… He was afflicted, yet He opened not His mouth.'[3]

We long for Christ's 'coming again'. Here we see how to wait in that longing, in the deep silence of prayerful waiting upon God.

---

[1] cf. Isa. 63: 9 (NKJV).
[2] Isa. 11: 2.
[3] Isa. 53: 7.

iv

Introduction

I notice with a feeling of wry recognition that Abba Agatho, when he first went into the desert, kept a stone in his mouth for three years, until he learnt to be silent. And here I am, struggling with words about silence. I must say what I can, and then go out and look for that stone!

To every opening line of the children's song, 'I like peace, I like quiet', my three sons used, when they were young, to reply rumbustiously, in word and deed, 'I like noise, I like riot'. Small wonder, then, that I am attracted to silence. Certainly I have found for a number of years that exploring silence in the context of the Christian tradition and the sacramental life is what gives my activity meaning.

One of my favourite stories is drawn from family life. It is the one about a mother who, against her better judgement, was showing her children an old-fashioned illustrated book of Christian stories. One picture was a particularly gruesome one of Christians being thrown to the lions. The mother was dismayed to see her three-year-old in tears. 'Oh dear', she said, 'what is the matter?' To which the child replied, 'Oh mummy, look, that poor little lion hasn't got a Christian.' This story seems to illustrate some of the necessary attitudes in any approach to prayer: that we should have a certain flexibility of expectation, and that we should be careful not to generalise about what other people may be experiencing. Don't do unto others as you would be done by, because others are different—as the proverb does not say. There are many ways of approach. What suits one might be quite wrong for another, and what works for us at one stage in our life might not always work. We need to be as flexible and open to the Holy Spirit as possible, without overlooking at the same time a need for the rhythm of habit and tradition and regularity. Prayer seems to me both an art, open to the deepest creative impulses in our being, and a discipline involving rhythm, accepting the systole and diastole, the ebb

1

and flow. Sometimes I need patiently to relax and allow things to happen, so that I can, as it were, see the space between the bars. At other times I need to find a framework, something upon which I can lean when times are bad; and equally, when a Pentecostal experience breaks through the old patterns and needs a deeper integration, there is the need to discover a new form.

Of one thing I am sure: that I find it easier to talk *to* God than I do to talk *about* God, and I know that I am not alone in this. The words no longer seem quite to fit for many people. We must take heart from a favourite saying of Eastern Orthodox Christians, 'The one who prays is a theologian, and the theologian is one who prays.' The living commitment to God is the first step in understanding. Between the *kerygma* (what is revealed in the Bible, Church and Tradition) and our existence (our daily experience in this century) falls a shadow. Many are finding that the old formulations are slipping from them and, in the words of Stevie Smith's poem,

> I was much too far out all my life
> And not waving but drowning.[1]

The image that often recurs in my mind is of myself climbing a familiar flight of stairs. A sudden stumble makes me reach out for support—only to find that the banisters are no longer there. Words without banisters. Are we then condemned to lives of quiet despair? I find help in the title of Fritz Schumacher's brilliant book *Small is Beautiful*. We must be prepared to start small from where we are, and not pine away with striving after the unattainable. We must stop struggling with words and meanings and restore a balance, spending more time exploring the silence from which words come.

---

[1] The poem 'Not Waving but Drowning' was published in *Not Waving But Drowning: Poems*, Stevie Smith, Andre Deutsch, 1957, and has been widely anthologised.

Approaching Silence

In a small way I have begun to find that the seeking of an inner silence in prayer provides a way which can sometimes heal and unite bits of me that seem a long way from each other. So much of our experience in life is tacit; words are only one means of communication. If words fail, let us look at other means and keep quiet until we find we have something to say. In some mysterious way, I think that what begins to happen is that not only do we begin to explore silence, but silence begins to explore us.

We are all battered by the noise and intrusiveness of our external environment, not only in terms of physical noise, but also in the assault on our capacity for sensitive concern, by all the sociological and psychological analysis, by the flow of televisual information and by ecological outrage. I think many of us are aware as never before of a need to counter-balance all this by being able to find an internal centre of gravity in the indwelling Christ, an inner fulcrum which might lift the world for us into the light of the eternal. We feel an urge to explore the possibilities of inner space, space which we sense must match in its vastness and mystery the images brought back by astronauts.

There are, of course, on all journeys in strange places, times when I panic and wish I'd never come—times when I'm sure that I've lost my passport, that I haven't acquired the necessary visas, and above all that I don't know the language and cannot communicate. I am suddenly vulnerable, exposed, dependent on finding someone to help, at the mercy of the 'unknown'. Yet for Christians the unknown is God himself. 'We are all in him enclosed', as Mother Julian says. Wherever the journey takes me, I cannot be taken out of God, provided I commit myself to God in faith, hope and love—even if the ways in which he leads me seem very strange to my understanding. If I find myself in dry deserts, or on vast, heaving oceans, or in the worst hells of the human mind, or just struggling on with my suburban existence, God is there. God promises that the Holy Spirit will never be refused as a source of inner strength to those who ask. I must ask and ask for a growing life in the Spirit until I can say with Job, 'though he slay me, yet will I trust in him'.[2] Always, however obscure to our eyes, there is around us and in us the possibility of joy in the vast 'more' of the Unknown—God himself—and the possibility of living a life of faith and trust in God.

Allowing Things to Happen

Once upon a time a village in China was suffering under a famine. The villagers had tried long and hard to produce rain by magic, witchcraft and ritual. At last they sent for a rainmaker from a distant village. In a few days a quiet little old man appeared. He settled down in a hut; he did what jobs needed to be done in and around the hut. And in three days the rain came. Sometimes all we can do in an intolerable situation is quietly to do the next thing, wait and allow things to happen—to be the kind of person around whom things *can* happen. (I admit that I do not always find it easy to distinguish between a wise passivity and my inveterate laziness and inertia, but the distinction needs to be made.)

In a book by the Jewish philosopher Martin Buber entitled *A Believing Humanism: Gleanings*,[3] there is a poem about Elijah. Buber uses the biblical events as images of Elijah's various states of mind as a prophet. Elijah would like to be a wind, blasting, blowing, stirring up:

> You sought me on your stormy paths,
> And did not find me.

---

[2] Job 13: 15 (NKJV).
[3] *A Believing Humanism: Gleanings*, Martin Buber, Simon & Schuster, 1969, p. 37.

He would like to have been a prophetic fire, burning, scorching and kindling:

> You sought Me in your flaming abysses
> And did not find Me.

It was not until he was overcome by silence, bowed to the earth in despair, that he became aware of deeper levels of his being and could allow things to happen, and then heard the voice of God in 'the hovering silence'.

An entry for 14 June 1843 in her journal by Caroline Fox, the Quaker, reads:

> It is the fuss and bustle principle which must proclaim itself until it is hoarse, that wars against Truth and Heroism. Let Truth be done in silence till it is forced to speak, and then, should it only whisper, all those whom it may concern will hear.[4]

Being Present Where We Are

One of the Jewish Hasidic tales is about Rabbi Isaac son of Yekel who lived in Cracow. He had a dream that under the pillar of a certain bridge in Prague treasure was to be found. So off he went to look for it. After he had been skulking about looking for an opportunity to dig, the guard on the bridge asked him what he was doing. Eventually he told him. The guard roared with laughter and said, 'Why, you silly man, you shouldn't take any notice of dreams. Only the other night I dreamt that in Cracow there was treasure hidden under the house of a Rabbi Isaac son of Yekel. Why, as you know, every second Rabbi is an Isaac son of Yekel'. But Rabbi Isaac son of Yekel went home.

God meets us where we are, and not where we are not, or when we are only half there. God dwells where we let him in.

---

[4] See generally *The journals of Caroline Fox, 1835–1871: a selection*, ed. Wendy Monk; London, Paul Elek, 1972.

In another Hasidic tale the Rabbi Zusya said, 'At the end I shall be asked, not, "Why were you not Moses?" but, "Why were you not Zusya?"'

We have to start with God where we are and as we are, and perhaps the difficulty which we all have in doing this can be the pivot that will enable us to 'turn' to God. I like the Hebrew word which Martin Buber loved to use, *teshuva*, meaning 'turning'—a strong and concrete physical image, the origin of our later ideas of repentance and penitence. The important thing is not what we feel but the fact that we turn to God and realise that there is always the possibility of transforming a situation through the 'turning'. At the very least it can turn bottomless despair into positive compunction, which can look up and out. A Rabbi was once asked, 'Why can we no longer hear the Word of God?' and the Rabbi answered, 'Because we can no longer stoop low enough to hear God's voice.'

Entering into Silence

Those of us who, in total dependence on the Holy Spirit, are seeking the contemplative way in the midst of a busy and unpredictable life, have to face the fact that the initial stages of 'tuning in' to silence are often very difficult. How can I cut through the constant pressure of my internal chatter into something deeper? We all have to experiment with various aids to find out which of them are most helpful to us. In these days of yoga, relaxation and psycho-prophylactic methods of childbirth, there is hardly need to mention that deep breathing and good posture can help—and are acquired only through teaching and practice.

I suspect that most of us find one of our senses more dominant than the others. If we can find a way of concentrating that one, then the rest will be held in check with it. For someone whose visual sense is strong it may help to let their eyes dwell on an icon or a crucifix, or on some symbol that holds the contradictions of life and its mysteries, and allow the truths they reveal to mediate themselves to us while we concentrate our attention gently on them, treating them as a window on to truth. Others find that reading for a while can help, using the words as a sort of 'audile icon' through which they can listen and hear the truth coming to them. I myself am what is known as a 'haptic' type (enjoying form with the implied sense of touch, as in sculpture); so I find that if I am feeling disintegrated I can concentrate myself best by best by running the knots in a piece of wool or string through my fingers, feeling the shape of each knot firmly and linking it with the repetition of a prayer or phrase. This is of course the rosary method, the 'Rose-garden Game' so well described in a book of that name by Eithne Wilkins. [5] Experience has convinced me that we must be open to new possibilities of ways in which the senses can lead us into silence and meaning. I remember once going to an exhibition of kinetics (works of art that make their impact through movement). I was admiring three forms that were standing still, close to each other, when someone pressed the button that set them in action. Suddenly I was oceans deep in the Trinity—three static forms became a unity through movement and interaction. Most of our models of the universe and of human behaviour are now dynamic, not static, and are governed by researches into communication and interaction. They often seem to me to present us with very vivid symbols for the divine activity and its interaction with the dynamics of human life.

I think for me it has been the gradual discovery of how to concentrate the faculties quietly through a dominant sense that has proved a way of pulling thought, feeling and

---

[5] *The Rose-Garden Game. The Symbolic Background to the European Prayer-Beads*, Eithne Wilkins, Victor Gollancz, 1969.

straying intuitions together so that I can begin, in the Quaker phrase, to 'centre down' and listen, look, stretch towards that which is beyond, in the silence.

There are times, of course, when one emotion is so dominant that I am drowned in it: an anxiety obsesses me; a depression darkens me; a joy unearths me. It is no good fighting with these states—the more I scold myself, the more stubborn they become. If the mood cannot be ignored then it has to be released, explored, opened out before God, not left travelling round the confines of my ego. This can be a difficult, painfully prolonged business if certain moods or states of mind simply do not shift. There may be something we cannot see for ourselves which is producing this state of mind. Perhaps one mood is masking another that we don't want to know about (for example, depression masking aggression, anxious conformity masking rebelliousness). We have to be sensible and recognise the times when we need to go to someone for help, or ask for their prayers. And if there does not seem to be anyone, then we must ask God to send someone. And God does.

I recognise that for those who are much more capable of pure thought than I am, there are times when thought must be pursued to its limit and held there in a state of balanced tension—the state that Simone Weil explores in her concept of *attente de Dieu*, waiting on God.

All of us know what it is to be tired, exhausted, grey with weariness, and at those times too we must allow ourselves, without strain, just to be like that, in the presence of God who knows and cares. After all, I am no less God's child asleep than awake. René Voillaume, in *Seeds of the Desert: Legacy of Charles de Foucauld*, describes what a real experience the prayer of tiredness has to become for the Little Brothers and Sisters of Jesus in the way they have chosen.[6] Perhaps our tiredness and weariness can be an offering we make to God for all the tiredness and weariness of our world, the sharing in prayer of the burdens of others who may know no source of strength.

Perhaps one of the more useful divisions of the world is that between introversion and extroversion. People do seem to vary between those who can most easily achieve a measure of silence by shutting their eyes and looking within and those whose best hope lies in focussing on an object outside themselves. Perhaps the introverted person, who has an active inner life, finds it easier to still the mind by looking away to the outside. Equally, the extrovert needs to look in, away from the excitement of external stimuli.

In regard to actual interruptions from outside, the most helpful attitude I have found occurs in one of the stories of the Desert Fathers. A man came and stayed with a hermit and apologised as he left for breaking in on the hermit's rule of life. The hermit replied, 'My rule is to receive you with hospitality and to let you go in peace.' Not all my friends would appreciate my phrasing it quite like that, but I take the point.

In his *A Pilgrim's Book of Prayers* Fr Gilbert Shaw provides a good summary of our attempts to enter into silence:

> The soul is inspired, instructed, and supported by the Holy Spirit, but its operations and knowledge are carried out and gained through the ordinary channels of its natural faculties. It must therefore use the powers which God has given it of perception, memory, understanding, emotional feeling, and imagination, so as to bring into activity its will to depend on God.[7]

Whatever preliminary exercises I may find helpful, they

---

[6] Anthony Clarke Books, 1972.
[7] *A Pilgrim's Book of Prayers*, Gilbert Shaw, SLG Press, 1992, Intro., p. xii.

are not an end in themselves, or ways of expanding my consciousness (though they may do so), but means towards establishing a unity of my being Godwards, of being at the disposal of God's presence, of being able to listen and to hear.

The Eternal Listener in Silence

In the Christian tradition silence is more often associated with the image of a listening companion than with a place emptied of sound. Learning to listen more to God is not, I suspect, very different from learning to listen more to my friends and neighbours. We probably all have to admit to sharing at times the tendency of the American writer and cartoonist James Thurber (1894-1961) not to listen when anybody else is talking, preferring to keep our mind a blank until they have finished and we can talk ourselves. Even more I recognise in myself the way in which a Scottish friend of ours says, 'I hear you, I hear you', when he means that he hears all right but does not intend to budge one inch in response.

Perhaps one could suggest several ways in which we might learn to listen to others. We can listen with a quality of relaxed attentiveness, so that the other knows that we are 'there' and yet not imposing our reactions too soon on whatever he or she may want to explore with us. Many things only take an actual shape for us in the atmosphere of trust provided by someone who really can and will listen. We can listen to what is said—to what is actually given, open and apparent between us in the situation—and respond with all that we are and can appropriately give at that moment; leaving the other free, and yet confirmed in their existence and potentiality. We can try to listen to what is *not* being said—what is being left out, hidden, kept back, not yet formulated—perhaps because there is not yet enough trust in our presence in the situation to allow certain things to be said. We must respond to that, too, with all the tacit sensitivity we have, in an enabling way, respecting to the uttermost the secrets and privacy of the other. Sometimes, too, we need to listen to the relationship itself, to what is going on at a deeper level between this 'other' and me. Are we using each other as objects rather than as real people? Are we getting at each other in some subtle, power-driven or masochistic way, so that we are very far from genuine encounter of the kind described so beautifully in a phrase of Rilke: 'Two solitudes that protect, touch and greet one another'? Then, also, from the deepest layers of our being, we can seek to listen to the beyond, the 'more', to that which is not yet immanent—we can listen towards the will of God.

I remember how my life was transformed during my professional training as a psychiatric social worker, when I realised how, by using words of exploration rather than of definition, one could open up new worlds of listening, learning and being, and create, as it were, a space in a relationship in which both people concerned could find more freedom to be, to express themselves, could have room to manoeuvre. In the context of listening, 'I wonder' seems to me a more creative phrase than 'I think' or 'I know'; so does the phrasing of thoughts as questions rather than as blunt statements which can force the other person into the position of having to reject or accept instead of being free to go on exploring. We all know that when we are feeling low and vulnerable, a rejection of what we say can feel very much like a rejection of us. Because they are grateful for our involvement, it is sometimes very difficult for persons who are dependent on us (however momentarily) as a listener to their problems, to reject outright something we say. How many of us have found ourselves in false situations in this way! We should always try to open a window rather than slam a door when we are called upon to listen very hard to someone in need. When we think of the tenderness and freedom God allows us, can we allow less to each other?

Beyond, beneath, within all our listening is the presence of the Eternal Listener, sustaining and enabling, listening in (and to) depths we shall never exhaust or fathom. This is no less true of our listening in prayer than of our listening to another human being.

Sifting Silence

I have said that it is sometimes silence that seems to explore us, to 'sift us', as the old Quakers used to say. There was said to be a strange sifting power in George Fox's silences. Once, for instance, he met with followers, testers and detractors in the country—and kept them for three hours while he sat in silence on a haystack. And they waited.

The silence sifts us because when we leave time and space in order to face what is inside us, we find out things we do not want to know. We have to learn to discover that things are different from what we thought; we might find, like the women after the Resurrection, the grave of our hopes empty and our true hope risen elsewhere, in a place in which we were not accustomed to look.

As a British art critic said of the women depicted in the cartoons of James Thurber: 'Inside every Little Nell there lurks a Lady Macbeth.' We have to learn to accept Lady Macbeth and find out how to live with her, neither letting her take control nor keeping her so repressed that she can only act secretly, as a saboteuse, poisoner and destroyer of what we value. She needs redemption. It is the story of Beauty and the Beast. We must learn to kiss the Beast in ourselves because God loves us totally and God's love can only change what we are prepared to acknowledge before him.

We have to hold on very hard in order to accept the depths of this search for the inner reality which silence explores in us. Areas of un-love are often hidden by dead, padlocked silences. We don't want to know, and yet we must. These are surely the times when it helps to know someone who will 'hold on' to God for us and with us when the struggle becomes overwhelming. It can overwhelm us at times, but the sea of love flows on if only we will let it. Perhaps at a much later date a little deep-sea diving can salvage unsuspected treasure from what we experienced at the time only as shipwreck.

Perhaps I would be guilty of what the existentialists call 'bad faith' if I left this in such a general form. For various reasons I have been trying to look at the theme of betrayal in my own 'beast'. We find the theme in well-known stories: Eden, Cain and Abel, Jacob and Esau, Saul, Samson, Job, Peter, Judas and Our Lord. There seems always to be a seed of betrayal in a relationship of trust; we can, after all, only betray and be betrayed by those we love. How easy it is to escape into thoughts of revenge, denial, cynicism or self-betrayal. Yet these experiences can expel us from an untried innocence into consciousness and responsibility. We have to grow up. If there were no betrayal we should never learn of the higher, transcendent forms of love experienced in forgiving and being forgiven. Love and forgiveness are not our possessions, they are gifts. Learning to face the betrayer and the betrayed in me can put me in touch with my need of these gifts, through my sorrow and suffering and my objective turning to God.

Many of us today are perplexed by the problem of violence and, here again, we need to find our own inner variant of the power-driven despot and the martyred victim who surface in bouts of irritation and mean-minded domestic tyranny. Sometimes it is only, as it were, by throwing things at God that we can discover the power of God to re-orientate our drive for power or martyrdom. Peter de Vries' astringent and moving novel *The Blood of the Lamb* is about a man brought up in the strict Calvinist tradition who tries to grow out of it and escape from it. His little daughter begins to die of leukaemia. Eventually he asks God that she might live one more year. The doctor announces that there has been a remission. On the way to the hospital with a cake to celebrate her birthday, the father hears that a chance bug has infected his daughter, and she dies very quickly. In utter dereliction of spirit he goes into a nearby church where he has sometimes reluctantly sheltered, to collect the cake which he had inadvertently left on a seat when he heard the news. On the way out, in a spasm of despair and rage, he throws the cake at the crucifix hanging with outstretched arms above the doorway. Suddenly he sees, through his tears, the patient hands of the crucified Christ move upwards and slowly and gently clear away the spattered mess, and a voice says: 'Suffer little children to come unto me.' And he finds himself, however momentarily, and against all the odds, at the foot of the Cross.[8]

The most difficult part of dealing with our Lady Macbeth is that we get things out of proportion and become distinctly humourless. As Kierkegaard said, the mountains within us labour together, and what do they bring forth? A mouse. But at least a timid little mouse is alive and real. I often take, as an image of what I am after, two wooden carvings I have of Don Quixote and Sancho Panza. There is Don Quixote, looking so tall, upright and righteous—asking for trouble—and there is Sancho Panza, relaxed, rounded and at ease on his horse, taking life with a sense of humour.

It is very difficult to talk about these subjects without appearing to be moralising and dreary. What we tend to look for are dramatic experiences, the timeless moments that do, thank God, happen. But all the great religious traditions,

---

[8] *The Blood of the Lamb: A Novel*, Peter De Vries, University of Chicago Press, 2005.

including our own, never cease to remind us of the need to 'keep on keeping on' in the nitty-gritty of the ascetical way, the eightfold path, or whatever metaphor each tradition uses. In the Christian tradition the aim has never been to gain self-awareness for its own sake, but through self-awareness to be able to abandon ourselves more completely to an awareness of the God who dwells within us. By virtue of that indwelling, God is deeply participant in our search, but is also that objective Reality towards which all our searchings for inner reality must move.

Shapes of Silence

We have to recognise that encountering the 'beast' is a lifetime's work, inextricably linked with all our experience of the mystery of good and evil. That heroic man, Alexander Solzhenitsyn, expresses it like this:

If only it were all so simple! If only there were evil people somewhere insidiously committing evil deeds, and it were necessary only to separate them from the rest of us and destroy them. But the line dividing good and evil cuts through the heart of every human being. And who is willing to destroy a piece of his own heart?

During the life of any heart this line keeps changing place; sometimes it is squeezed one way by exuberant evil and sometimes it shifts to allow enough space for good to flourish. One and the same human being is, at various ages, under various circumstances, a totally different human being. At times he is close to being a devil, at times to sainthood. But his name doesn't change, and to that name we ascribe the whole lot, good and evil.[9]

---

[9] *The Gulag Archipelago 1918-1956: An Experiment in Literary Investigation I-II*, Alexander Solzhenitsyn, trans. Thomas P. Whitney, Book Club Associates, 1974, p.168.

15

If we find that we are still on the journey into silence, in spite of many setbacks, then silence begins to create its own shapes inside us. I want here to look at four shapes of silence beautifully described by Ivan D. Illich in his essay, 'The Eloquence of Silence'.[10] He points out that if we wish to learn a language, it is as important to hear the silences in it as to know the words. He likens language to a cord of silence, with words as the knots. The silence and the sounds together produce the particular rhythm of the language.

The silence of availability. This is the experience of necessary passivity, availability. The word is conceived and rooted in silence. We need to expose ourselves to the creative Spirit: 'Be it unto me'; 'Here am I'.

The silence of growth. This is the silence of gestation, the internal growth and nurture of the word after conception. We have to close in to prepare the word for its eventual birth at the proper moment. This is the silence before and between words: prayer in which words have the courage to swim in a sea of silence.

Silence beyond words. This is pure silence, after words have done all they can, the silence of lovers. This is the origin and completion of all words when 'we must aim at that Silence which alone God is in himself'.

The silence of the Pietà. This is the silence of suffering and the mystery of death. This is not the passive acceptance of the Word of God—*Fiat*; nor the manly acceptance of Gethsemane—obedience; it is the mysterious silence in which God can descend into hell, the silence of freely-willed powerlessness, the self-emptying of God, the fulfilment of the mystery of the Incarnation.

---

[10] The essay is in *Celebration of Awareness: A Call for Institutional Revolution,* Ivan D. Illich, Penguin Education Special, Penguin Books, 1973.

All these and other shapes of silence we may find coming to us in image, symbol, story, icon—gradually making their own room inside us if only we let them. Small is beautiful. Sometimes we have to spend a long time nursing one small truth until we receive another. 'It is required that those who have been given a trust must prove faithful.'[11]

Enduring Silence

I think the inner discipline of the practice of silent prayer can help us to endure in the face of much doubt and disturbance of our faith. If absolute faith were always possible it would hardly be faith. Carrying our own share of honest doubt is surely part of the journey into a living faith. The process of carrying our faith and our doubt seems to me to need a good deal of honest silence and endurance, as well as the search for meaning in words. In Isaiah, silence and hope appear to be specially linked. Where there is silence there is a nesting place for hope—pure hope; not hope of anything in particular—just *hope.*

Also, and this is the other side of the coin, there is no doubt that silence needs to be endured with an incredible amount of patience and quiet persistence. The image of a journey that we so often use in speaking of the spiritual life can be misleading if it predisposes us to think that we should always be on the move, that something should be 'happening'. The forty years in the wilderness can hardly have seemed a journey; a grim endurance test, more likely, with everyone needing all their strength just to plod on, so as not to slide down a spiral of hopelessness and despair. There are times in prayer when the desert seems gritty, refreshing water is short, Brother Camel—the body—has 'got the hump', and there is little to be done but pull the blanket over our heads and sit it out, and not go sloping off after some tempting mirage.

---

[11] 1 Cor. 4: 2 (NIV).

17

Living with Silence

Often when we turn from our own subjective experiencing towards God we find ourselves saying, 'Truly you are a God who hides himself.'[12] God appears to be silent, so silent as to frighten us into thinking that God has gone.

We must first try to discover to what extent we are being like Oedipus—who plucked out his eyes and then cried against the dark. Using a similar image Catherine of Genoa said: 'If a person would see properly in spiritual matters, let them pluck out the eyes of their own presumption.' But without the eyes of presumption we often feel blind indeed. I sometimes find that seeking silence and self-awareness can lead into a dark inner apathy, a sort of vacuum which sucks into itself all one's most dire egotism. Then we can become absorbed in the illusions and idolatries woven by our self-reflecting narcissism.

On the other hand, the dark unknownness of God and the silence of God are very much a mysterious part of Christian experience for which it is difficult to find adequate words. I know that I have been helped in struggling with this not only by the apophatic[13] tradition of Eastern Orthodoxy but also by Martin Buber, the great Jewish philosopher. He was sure that people in the present age have confined God too much to their own subjectivity, losing God in the convolutions of their own psyches. We have abandoned the life of faith and sold ourselves out to forms of what he called 'psychological gnosticism', to an 'I know' attitude, where we are more concerned with power and knowledge than with love and trust. He was also sure that we have become too impersonal

---

[12] Isa: 45: 15 (NRSV).

[13] From *apophasis*—negation, denial. Apophatic theology is that kind which denies all attributes to God such as goodness, wisdom, majesty, simplicity, in order, as Gregory Palamas says, 'to draw near to the Unknown in the darkness of absolute unknowing'.

about what lies outside ourselves. The result is that we lack spontaneity and cannot step into relationship with the Living God. We must, Buber said, begin to penetrate existence by active love; then we would find the signs of God were there: they are spoken into life, not above it.

In an essay called 'At the Turning', Buber talks of the age-old Jewish cry, 'Will He allow injustice to reign further'?

How is life with God still possible in a time in which there is an Auschwitz? ... The estrangement has become too cruel, the hiddenness too deep ... dare we urge the survivors, 'Call to him for he is kind; his mercy endures forever'?[14]

Of Job he writes:

And he receives an answer from God. But what God says to him does not answer the charge, it does not even touch upon it. The true answer Job receives is God's appearance only, only this, that distance turns into nearness, that his eyes 'see him'. Nothing is explained; nothing adjusted; wrong has not become right; nor cruelty, kindness. Nothing has happened but that man again hears God's address.

How is it with us? do we stand overcome before the hidden face of God? ... No, rather even now we contend, we too, with God ... though his coming appearance resemble no earlier one, we shall recognise again our cruel and merciful Lord.

Presence in Silence

So then, if we can do without the explanations and the adjustments, we are able to experience prayer as an unending pursuit of the Presence. Then silence is the place of the Presence, and at its heart is God.

---

[14] Essay 'At the Turning' in *At the Turning: Three Addresses on Judaism*, Martin Buber, Farrar, Strauss & Young, 1952.

God's presence cannot be conjured or constrained, but if we wait upon him—a waiting that might mean asking, seeking, knocking, or *just waiting*—in faith, hope and love, we shall see what is given us to see. Buber points out that Moses did not see God's face, but he learnt his ways. Our Lord's face may be obscure, but we know his ways—of love and justice and self-emptying—and we see him in our neighbours, who need our caring and our prayers.

How can we speak of that mysterious Presence at the heart of silence? Perhaps only through the cherishing of his Name and its mysteries. The real Hebrew meaning, we are told, of the mystery of the Name, rendered in our biblical versions as 'I am that I am', should be, 'I shall be there as I shall be there'. God's presence is assured; the form it will take is not. If we wish to recognise the form of the Living God in each moment, then we must keep close and be watchful with the love of all our heart, mind and strength. The great forms or images of God were born of encounter, and they change: You are this… and yet not this…

That great and humble man, George Appleton, at one time Archbishop in Jerusalem, expressed this way of approach in one of his prayers:

O Christ, my Lord, again and again
I have said with Mary Magdalene,
'They have taken away my Lord
and I know not where they have laid him.'
I have been desolate and alone.
And thou hast found me again, and I know
that what has died is not thou, my Lord,
but only my idea of thee,
the image which I have made to preserve
what I have found, and to be my security.
I shall make another image, O Lord,
better than the last.

That too must go, and all successive images,
until I come to the blessed vision of thyself,
O Christ my Lord.[15]

The movement into deeper silence will always bring us into touch with the mysteries of life and human experience: suffering, death, love, evil. We need to bear in mind a distinction, drawn by Gabriel Marcel in his book, *Being and Having*, between those problems one can face and work on, recognising them as ultimately soluble, and those problems which are mysteries, yielding their meaning only according to the quality of being we are able to bring to them.

There come times when inner silence is experienced as an utter void. God is not only the firm ground and substance of my being, but also the abyss. The silence is no longer me-shaped, but infinitely God-shaped. It is a terrible thing to fall into the hands of the Living God (even if, as has been said, it is a worse thing to fall out of them). The abyss takes us in an absolutely real way into the meaning of the phrase, 'the fear of the Lord'. Like St Patrick and his Trinitarian breastplate, we need something to which to bind ourselves—the Prayer of the Name: 'Lord Jesus Christ, Son of the living God, have mercy on me, a sinner'; 'My God and my all'; or some other rhythmical prayer, can be a boat in which to embark on the deeper seas of silence. We can entrust ourselves to it; we can lash ourselves to it when the seas are rough, or rest in it when becalmed.

The tradition and teaching associated with the Jesus Prayer in the Orthodox Church is very rich. To put it briefly, from where I stand I call upon the Name of the Lord (neither, it is said, can I call him Lord unless the Spirit calls through me), *Lord Jesus Christ ... have mercy on me* in all the mysteries

---

[15] *The Oxford Book of Prayer*, ed. George Appleton, Oxford University Press, 1985, no. 498, p. 147.

of my created being; *have mercy on me, a sinner.* At ever new
depths I turn in wonder and dependence on the mysteries of
the Trinity and the Incarnation. And from the depths of the
abyss into which that plunges me, again I turn and call *Lord*
... to immerse myself once more in the Source of the
mysteries of the faith.

There is a phrase, *nexus mysteriorum*, once much used, I
believe, which is an attempt to express the internal
consistency and inter-relatedness of the ultimate mysteries of
the world. The Jesus Prayer is certainly one of the ways in
which we can experience this nexus. The movement of the
prayer is infinite because it increasingly puts in the heart of
our being the silent heart of all being, the divine Name. And
the whole offering in the prayer is the same movement that
we experience in the Eucharist and in all sacramental living,
and is never, in the Christian tradition, separated from them.

Martin Buber met many people who experienced
difficulty in using the word 'God'. I want to quote a passage
where he responds to this difficulty:

'Yes,' I said, 'it is the most heavily-laden of all human
words. None has become so soiled, so mutilated. Just for
this reason I may not abandon it. Generations of men
have laid the burden of their anxious lives upon this
word and weighed it to the ground; it lies in the dust
and bears their whole burden. The races of man with
their religious factions have torn the word to pieces; they
have killed for it and died for it, and it bears their finger-
marks and their blood. Where might I find a word like it
to describe the highest! If I took the purest, most
sparkling concept from the inner treasure-chamber of the
philosophers, I could only capture thereby an unbinding
product of thought. I could not capture the presence of
Him whom the generations of men have honoured and
degraded with their awesome living and dying. I do
indeed mean Him whom the hell-tormented and heaven-

storming generations of men mean. Certainly they draw caricatures and write "God" underneath; they murder one another and say, "In God's name". But when all madness and delusion fall to dust, when they stand over against Him in the loneliest darkness and no longer say "He, He" but rather sigh "Thou", shout "Thou", all of them the one word, and when they then add "God", is it not the real God whom they all implore, the One Living God, the God of the children of man? Is it not He who *hears* them? And just for this reason is not the word "God", the word of appeal, the word which has become a *name*, consecrated in all human tongues for all times? We must esteem those who interdict it because they rebel against the injustice and wrong which are so readily referred to "God" for authorisation. But we must not give it up. How understandable it is that some suggest we should remain silent about the "last things" for a time in order that the misused words may be redeemed! But they are not to be redeemed *thus*. We cannot cleanse the word "God" and we cannot make it whole; but, defiled and mutilated as it is, we can raise it from the ground and set it over an hour of great care.'[16]

The Presence, within us and yet totally beyond us, is not an alien intrusive force but can become perceptible to us as a living Person with whom we enter into dialogue—what Buber called 'dialogically perceivable'. How much we can learn from the Old Testament patriarchs as they argue with God; and from the Psalms when the speaker changes his attitude through being prepared to enter into honest dialogue and say what is going on inside! I think we have to relearn what is meant by asking. It is not bullying or cajoling, nor is it falling over backwards to say, 'far be it from me…, but…' It is learning the simplicity of a dependence that *can* ask.

---

[16] *Eclipse of God: Studies in the Relation between Religion and Philosophy*, Martin Buber, Victor Gollanz, 1953, I. Prelude: Report on Two Talks, pp. 17-18.

Shared Silence

Although the journey into God is one that we must each undertake individually, in ever-increasing depth, yet we know that we are also called together; we need each other, we are inescapably part of each other. My want is part of the want of the whole. My peace, joy, search, need, are part of the whole. One of Buber's main insights is that of 'the between'. God, the eternal Thou, is not the possession of any of us, but is experienced 'between us' in any genuine meeting.

Yet how do we find a meaningful outward expression of this *koinonia*, fellowship, when so many of the organised structures fail to satisfy deeply-felt needs? Some of us have found that to explore silence in prayer in small groups is a help. I realised what an upholding and strengthening experience this could be when I shared in the prayer hours of a contemplative community and felt it was a pity this sort of sharing was not more widely attempted outside such communities. I had also been a Friend (Quaker) and had learnt that it was possible to maintain a disciplined and meaningful form of meeting in which silence was the binding factor. I believe that in the discipline and depth of silence we can begin to come into a quite new, living relationship with the silent, unknown shapes of God, the God who speaks through silences. I think this actual sharing can also take us into a new awareness of being part of the Communion of Saints. Fr Gilbert Shaw, again in his *Pilgrim's Book of Prayers*, says:

> It is natural to our loneliness and fitting to our humility to ask the prayers and care of our friends. It would be indeed unneighbourly if we restricted this operation to the limited circle of those whom we could know in the flesh, and ignored the number of those whom we might come to know by faith.[17]

---

[17] *A Pilgrim's Book of Prayers*, op. cit., p. xx.

Philosophers like Michael Polanyi have sought to show that much of our knowledge is based on what he calls, in his book of that name, 'the tacit dimension'. In both Christian and Jewish traditions there are moving descriptions of encounters between people in which shared communication through silence meant more than words could ever express. There is the famous meeting between St Louis, King of France, and Brother Egidio, the Franciscan. They had longed to meet; when they did they embraced, remained long in silence, and parted. Brother Egidio was asked why they did not speak and replied:

> from the minute we embraced, the light of divine wisdom showed his heart to me and mine to him. By the workings of God we looked into each other, knowing what I wanted to say to him and what he wanted to say to me better and with greater comfort than if we had spoken. Because of the inadequacy of all words, which cannot clearly express the secret mysteries of God, there would have been disappointment rather than comfort.[18]

And then there is the delightful Hasidic tale of Rabbi Mendel of Vorki. Rabbi Mendel and his Hasidim once sat at table in silence. The silence was so deep that a fly on the wall could be heard. After the meal a visiting Rabbi said to his neighbour, 'What a table we had today. I was probed so deeply that I thought my veins would burst, but I managed to hold my own and answer every question I was asked!' Rabbi Mendel lived in a period of Hasidic decline when people felt immersed in a dark and corrupt time. For him silence was the way, a living and effective force.

Some of the animal ethologists make very interesting assessments that we might do well to meditate upon. Robert Ardrey, in his book *The Social Contract*, writes this:

---

[18] *The Little Flowers of St Francis*, Brother Ugolino, Part I, ch. XXIV.

The just society, as I see it, is one in which sufficient order protects members, whatever their diverse endowments, and sufficient disorder provides every individual with opportunities to develop his genetic endowment, whatever that may be.[19]

He also points out that diversity is the material of evolution and that the pursuit of security (and conformity) is only reward-bearing if you do not have it.

Those of us who do meet in groups, with the sharing of silent prayer at the heart of them, need to be aware of fruitful tensions between protection and development, diversity and risk, if we do not want to become institutionalised in the wrong sense. Thomas Merton says somewhere that to become a personality you have to be exclusive; in order to become a mature human being you have to be inclusive. Something of the same nature surely applies to our group experiences.

Yet at the same time, while being flexible, we have to be disciplined about what goes on. Are we there for a therapeutic purpose or not? If we are going into the field of trying to cope with psychological problems directly, then we must know a great deal about group dynamics and recognise that some people only feel real when they are the centre of attention. But it seems to me that if we can curb our natural curiosity and our desire to be involved and to help, a simple acknowledgement of need, and a lifting of it to God, provides a middle way by which we can best help each other. There is an obvious danger that if we are not disciplined then the strongest or the sickest psyche may dominate the atmosphere of the group, leading to great difficulties and psychic contamination, and the true interior development of the many may be cramped or crippled. I doubt whether a silent prayer group is the right place for very sick souls and perhaps we

---

[19] *The Social Contract: A Personal Inquiry into the Evolutionary Sources of Order and Disorder*, Robert Ardrey, Dell Publishing, 1974, p. 3.

should be rigorous about this early enough and not allow the situation to get out of hand. There are other occasions for the active expression of love and concern.

There is an idea around that members of a group should be experiencing a 'high' most of the time. This, of course, is nonsense. Life is not all 'highs', and plateaux are as important as peaks. I think that it can sometimes help to put into words, simply, in conversation afterwards, the 'feeling' of the silence: 'Sticky tonight', or 'helpful tonight'. This can enable the less experienced members to go away without a sense of guilt and 'It's all me' about it. Of course there are bad patches, and we must watch the quality of what we are sharing. There is the story of the old countryman who, faced with a Quaker meeting, said, 'What's the good of going to hear them as has nowt to say?' That can be balanced against another remark: 'If they'd said anything I could have answered them.'

I would like to recall two Quaker accounts of the positive value of corporate silence. Friends, after all, have been sharing silence for a long time. The first is that of Caroline E. Stephen in 1908:

> In the united stillness of a truly 'gathered' meeting there is a power known only by experience, and mysterious even when most familiar.[20]

The second account is from the Scottish Quaker convert of the seventeenth century, Robert Barclay:

> Not by strength of arguments or by a particular disquisition of each doctrine, and convincement of my understanding thereby, came [I] to receive and bear witness of the Truth, but by being secretly reached by [the] Life. For, when I came into the silent assemblies of God's people, I felt a secret power among them, which

---

[20] *Light Arising: Thoughts on the Central Radiance*, Caroline E. Stephen, 1908, pp. 68-69.

touched my heart; and as I gave way unto it I found the evil weakening in me and the good raised up; and so I became thus knit and united unto them, hungering more and more after the increase of this power and life whereby I might feel myself perfectly redeemed; and indeed this is the surest way to become a Christian; to whom afterwards the knowledge and understanding of principles will not be wanting.[21]

There can be in a shared silence something that strengthens, upholds, teaches us, once we realise that it is not just a case of tolerating each other's waywardness but a turning in love together to that which unites us—the presence of God.

Conclusion

I will end by quoting a rhythmic prayer, 'Seeking Wholeness', which Mother Mary Clare SLG adapted from a section of *The Face of Love* by Fr Gilbert Shaw:

> Most loving Lord, hold me fast to live by you
> > in all occasions of my life,
> > > in the busyness of daily life and in my sleeping hours.

> Keep my heart united to yourself
> > to be the temple of the Holy Spirit
> > > that he revealing you to me

---

[21] Robert Barclay (1648-90), quoted in *Quaker Faith and Practice: The Book of Christian Discipline of the Yearly Meeting of the Religious Society of Friends (Quakers) in Britain*, Quaker Peace & Service, 4th ed., 2009, 19: 21.

may energise my soul
to be more fully one with you.

If I forget you in the manifold confusions
    of all the outward passing things,
    still the inmost depths of memory and will
    that all my thinking may return
    to know that you indwell my heart.

Cleanse the complex patterns of my unconsciousness
    that nothing may distort my will
    or turn my heart from loving you,
    from serving you in spirit and in truth.

May every thought and action of the day
    be unified and offered to your praise;
    and while I sleep may my heart wake,
        giving unto you my love
        to glorify your name,
    that all that is not wholly reconciled to you
    may be resolved and simplified by love,
    the love which is the knowledge of yourself.

Look well, O soul, upon yourself
    lest spiritual ambition
    should mislead and blind you
    to your essential task—
        to wait in quietness:
        to knock and persevere in humble faith.

Knock; knock in love,
>*nor fail to keep your place before the door*
>*that when Christ wills—and not before—*
>*he may open unto you the treasures of his love.*

Grant me therefore humility of soul
>that I may grow in penitence
>dependent on the Holy Spirit's light.

BIBLIOGRAPHICAL NOTES

All Rabbinic and Hasidic tales in this paper are in *Tales of the Hasidim* (two vols: *The Early Masters* and *Later Masters*), Martin Buber, Schocken Books, first published 1947 and 1948 respectively.

Teaching on the Jewish understanding of the Divine Name (p. 20) is contained in Martin Buber's books *I and Thou*, trans. Walter Kaufmann, T. & T. Clark Ltd., 1971, and *The Prophetic Faith*, Harper Torchbooks, 1960. See also 'Buber's understanding of the Divine Name related to Bible, Targum and Midrash' by Pamela Vermes in the *Journal of Jewish Studies*, 24:2 (Autumn 1973).

A classic exposition of the Jesus Prayer in Orthodox spirituality is to be found in Kallistos Ware's *The Power of the Name*, SLG Press, 1974 (available from SLG Press). There is a very useful introduction by the same author in *The Art of Prayer: An Orthodox Anthology*, Igumen Chariton of Valamo, trans. E. Kadloubovsky and G. E. H. Palmer, Faber & Faber, 1971. Another helpful short work is *On the Invocation of the Name of Jesus* by a Monk of the Eastern Church (Lev Gillet), Fellowship of St Alban and St Sergius, 1960.

George Appleton's book, *One Man's Prayers*, SPCK 1977, contains many prayers which express a profound ability to grapple with the secular insights of our day, for instance in the field of psychology, combined with a deep living faith in the objective reality of God and the need for our personal commitment and response to God.

Gilbert Shaw's books, *A Pilgrim's Book of Prayers* and *The Face of Love*, both originally published by A. R. Mowbray, are published by SLG Press. For current availability, and for e-book editions, see www.slgpress.co.uk